SINGLE AGAIN!

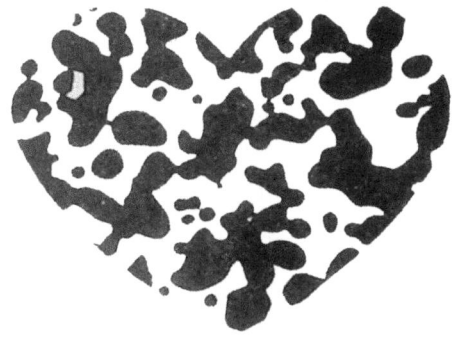

NOT BY CHOICE!

SINGLE AGAIN!

NOT BY CHOICE!

Lana E. Bach

CITIOFBOOKS, INC.
3736 Eubank NE Suite A1
Albuquerque, NM 87111-3579
www.citiofbooks.com

Printed in the United States of America.

ISBN-13: Paperback   979-8-89391-507-5
           eBook   979-8-89391-508-2

Library of Congress Control Number: 2025900730

I dedicate this book to my loving family and friends who cared, encouraged, and supported me during the most difficult trial of my entire life.

To my Christian counselor, Rob, I say "thank you" for enduring those sessions when I repeated myself over and over again!

But especially to my husband, Steven Arthur, who also knows the pain of divorce and being single not by choice. Thank you, honey, for loving me, supporting me, understanding me and giving so much of yourself to me… I love you!

Thank you, my Heavenly Father, for the new life you have given me, and for your unfailing love for me!

CONTENTS

FOREWORD

BY REV. STEVEN A. BACH

My dear "brown eyes," thank you Lana, for telling your story of hope and recovery from complete brokenness and devastation.

Those of us who have walked the path of midnight darkness can understand the pain. Yet, we can also share an encouraging word to those who are in the same valley of despair.

This book conveys such honesty and insight on some practical steps that can bring healing to the mind and restoration to the soul.

There is no doubt, in my mind, that this book will be read over, and over again, then passed on to others who need to know that life is still worth living.

Honey, I am proud of you for all the effort you put into this book. I know the depth of your love and I thank God for blessing me by being your husband.

PREFACE

A friend of mine had learned that his wife was unfaithful to him. She told him that she no longer loved him. He was found dead the next day, hanging in his basement.

What a sad ending to a life for which God had such a wonderful plan! If only he had given God a chance!

INTRODUCTION

*M*y most important goal in writing this book is to help those who are in pain to know that God isn't finished with their lives. Even though we don't understand, God does. My hope in sharing my experiences of pain, perseverance, growth and victory with others is that they will know that God can restore the joy and happiness of life to them!

I hope this book will help you understand that there are others who have experienced the pain you may be feeling at this very moment.

If you hold on to God's truth, stay faithfully obedient to Him, and remain a yielded vessel, God will get you through! He will take your situation and turn it into something good. You can become a better person (Job 23:10, Psalm 66:10) and have a much deeper relationship with God.

God will give you the strength that you need as you need it (Philippians 4:13) and give you the peace to sleep at night (Psalm 29:11, Psalm 91:1, Matthew 11:28). I cannot begin to tell you how glad I am that I didn't pull the trigger on my gun that wintery day! Now, less than five years later, I am sitting on a couch in my lovely home, with a husband who loves me, and whom I love dearly, writing this book to YOU!

See, God is still God, and you are still you! God is not finished with your life! Let him do what He does best – take what seems impossible and make it into more than possible! He will change you from victim to victor!

CHAPTER 1

THERE WAS NOTHING TO LIVE FOR

I still remember the feelings and terrible emotions that tormented me as I was lying face down on the floor in the corner of my upstairs bedroom. The wrenching pain in my heart was more than I could bear! It never let up for months. I had come to the conclusion that the pain would always be there. The winter sun was shining through the window warming my body as I pointed the gun to my head.

The grief was more than I could bear. My life would never be the same - how could it? I'd had the perfect life, or so I thought. I became a Christian at age nine, attended a "Full Gospel" Church, enjoyed ministering with youth and evangelism teams. My husband would love me for the rest of my life, or so I thought!

All the hopes I had for a wonderful life in the future were shattered when, after 15 years of marriage, my husband informed me that he had never loved me and had filed for a divorce. I couldn't believe what I was hearing on that night he so coldly spoke those words that cut my heart out.

He was a "Christian" and this kind of thing wasn't supposed to happen to Christians! Besides, he'd said he loved me and I loved him dearly. I had given him over 15 of the best years of my life! I wanted us to grow old together! But none of that mattered and now there was nothing to live for. I was now a victim of divorce!

DIVORCE! A word that I thought would never apply to my life was now tearing my heart apart. I have seen others go through this kind of devastation but, Lord, not me!

I dreaded the loneliness to come each day and night, the memories of the past each time I would walk by a hugging couple, the embarrassment of my marriage's supposed "failure," the pain of those constant piercing words, "I never loved you," and most of all, having to establish a new life at age 35! I knew I couldn't take it.

"God, if you don't end this pain for me, I will do it for you," I kept repeating over and over to myself as I lay weeping on my bedroom floor. I cried so long I didn't even have enough energy to sigh one more tear.

I remember the battle that went on in my mind and soul as I said to myself "Pull the trigger! God doesn't care! End the pain! But at the same time, a still and gentle voice tenderly spoke to me saying "God will get you through. Don't end what God is still working on. He promised to be with you…" I struggled in my mind with the truth.

All I knew was that I had loved and served Christ since I was age nine. I was faithful to my husband and to God. I had served as a church secretary for seven years, became involved with short term missions, Sunday school teaching, evangelism outreaches, drama ministry, and I loved all of it!

I was taught that God answered prayers, and I have seen so many prayers answered, but where was God now? I prayed and fasted for my husband to have a change of heart about the divorce, but the situation only worsened. I couldn't believe that God wasn't answering my desperate prayers as I cried out to Him at this most devastating time in my life! I didn't understand how my husband, who claimed to be a Christian, could turn into a person I barely even knew. Christians weren't supposed to get divorced! God HATES divorce! What did I do to deserve this? What could I do to save this marriage? Did my husband even want to save our marriage? What was the truth?

I was lying on my bedroom floor, thoughts whirling in my mind, my finger on the trigger of a .25 Caliber Baretta. I am convinced now that the angles of God caused me to fall asleep and kept me from pulling the trigger on that dreadful, cold, wintery day. The next thing I knew, I woke up to the sound of my doorbell ringing. I now thank God for keeping me from the devil's attempt that day to end my life! I had no right to end a life that God wasn't through with, even if it was my own! Now, years later, I know that I had much to live for, and God really was with me during that dark, cold time in my life.

CHAPTER 2
"WHY ME GOD? WHAT DID I DO WRONG?"

*T*hat horrible scene in my life will always be very real to me. Sometimes I have flashbacks of that heart wrenching time in my life. I know there are those of you who are reading this book who can relate to the pain of divorce: the agony of being a "victim," and unable to control the painful circumstances of divorce in your life.

In my despair, I wrote a letter to a dear pastor of mine who had transferred out of state just when I discovered the tides of my marriage had turned toward divorce. I would like you to read a portion of this letter:

"Dear Pastor,

I so appreciate your counsel and prayers when you phoned me. I feel so desperate and lost at this point... He said he was tired of me and he was not in love with me anymore.

My heart breaks every time I think of how I thought we would grow old together and have a future to share. I truly love him! I have been trying to get him to change his mind. But he has his mind set on divorce.

I feel so abandoned by everyone and, at times, I feel that even God cannot hear me. I am trying to find a church where no one will know me, so I don't have to face all the questions and heartache. I hope you will continue to pray for us.

It hurts when someone you love does not return the love you are dishing out. Am I a fool for doing this, Pastor?

Well, I can't tell you how much I need your prayers. I never thought I would ever have to go through a divorce! You know me... I always like to make sure of everything... and here, the most important person in my life has decided that he doesn't want me anymore. I feel I'm in a slow torture.

But, I know whom I have believed in! I am sure that God will make good out of his situation, right, Pastor? Please let me know if you have any suggestions for me, o.k.?

Please forgive the bad news. I wish it could have been better..."

How true those feelings were at the time. God kept me through those trying months of agony. Anyone who has gone through this trauma knows the degree that we suffer is also the degree of how real God can be to us! I never drew closer to God in all my life than during that desperate time in my life. The realm of relationship I began to develop with God was totally different from anything I ever had before! He was my best friend and even the little things that He did for me meant so much!

The intense pain and rejection I felt for months were worse than anything I had ever experienced. The questions that kept rolling through my mind haunted me every minute of the day for months!

Any time a person is rejected by someone he or she loves, the question will be asked over, and over again, "What did I do wrong?" But I discovered that human beings are not alone in this question, and that even God asked in Jeremiah 2:5 (NIV) *"What fault did your fathers find in me, that they strayed so far from me?"* Our perfect Father in heaven, who does NO WRONG, asked the same question that I asked, and many others ask themselves, during a time of rejection – "What did I do wrong?"

In reality, you may have done absolutely nothing to warrant the kind of treatment you received from that loved one. In asking myself the question of "What did I do wrong?" over and over again, I have come to some sound conclusions.

First, the scenario of divorce – whatever the reason, someone breaks covenant – is often a result of one or more person's selfishness and lack of relationship with God. In seeking God for an answer to that question, I found God leading me to this scripture in II Timothy 3:1-4 (NIV) "But mark this: There will be terrible times in the last days. **People will be lovers of themselves**, lovers of money, boastful, proud, abusive, disobedient to their parents, ungrateful, unholy, without love, unforgiving, slanderous, without self-control, brutal, not lovers of good, treacherous, rash, conceited**, lovers of pleasure rather than lovers of God."**

I know you have been a faithful spouse and given the best you can to that person who has decided that he no longer wants to be married to you. We find the answer to that haunting question, "What did I do wrong?" in the scriptures given to us in II Timothy.

Sinful human nature will always lead to destruction unless that nature is turned over to God. Human nature is to be "selfish," "lovers of self," lovers of pleasure rather than lovers of God." Is it any wonder that one out of every two marriages in America is ending in divorce? Christians are NOT exempt from human nature!

7

Friend, any one of us has the ability to follow our own desires when we stray from our relationship with God. I believe this is what Paul meant in I Corinthians 15:31: *"I die daily..."* Keeping our hearts in tune, loving God, and loving one another requires constant check and balance! When even one of the two people required to make a marriage decides (and that is what it is: a decision) not to keep the check and balance system in tune with God, it will result in human nature ruling one's life. Thus, those who are closest to that person will feel the brunt of their decision to "do his own thing." In *"dying daily,"* you surrender your will to the will of God.

Secondly, if almighty God, who is perfect in every way, was rejected by man, doesn't it go without saying that some people will NEVER be pleased? It is hard to understand "Why?" when you are the one being rejected. Take comfort in knowing that even God asked the question "What did I do wrong?" in the book of Jeremiah – you are not alone! God completely understands the feeling of giving total love and then being rejected. Sin not only affects the sinner, but also, those who love the sinner, especially God. Even giving your very life for someone does not guarantee his love and devotion to you in return.

I don't believe in sharing details or glorifying anyone's sin! Therefore, I don't want to give details of how or why my husband said he left me, except to say I KNOW THE FEELINGS!

I know the feeling that comes over you when your spouse announces that he is filing for divorce. I know the nights of waiting up late watching each television station go off the air while hoping that my husband would soon come back home.

Every time the phone rang, I felt the anxiety of wishing for it to be him on the other end of the line. I know the feeling of loneliness when I had to eat each meal alone, even when I begged my husband to have dinner with me. I know the feeling of suspicion and lack of control when the phone rings and another female voice is on the other end asking to speak to my husband one more time.

I know the feeling of longing and wet tears that drenched my pillow during the midnight hours, alone in bed wondering where he was and when this nightmare would end.

The words "for richer or for poorer, in sickness and in health, **until death do us part**" no longer produced the secure feeling of love I once had in my life.

The stress and confusion in my mind were so great that I had to seek professional help. I thank God for Rob, my Christian counselor, who sat patiently with me session after session listening to me "spill my guts".

During one of the counseling sessions I had with Rob, I asked him a question that had been nagging at me since the divorce trial began: "Why doesn't God make my husband come back to me?" I told my counselor how I had been praying and fasting, begging God to MAKE my husband come back – and God wasn't answering my prayers! Why?

I'll never forget the answer my very wise and godly counselor gave me, and I have since shared with many who have asked the same question. He said, "Lana, God is a great God, but there is one thing that He does not do, and that is force His will on people! It is every man's choice as to whether he follows God or doesn't follow God". *("If any man chooses to do God's will…" John 7:17 NIV)* That statement set me free from thinking God didn't hear me or stopped caring for me.

God can do everything to make circumstances such that one will have the mind set to repent and follow God's way. But God will NEVER force a person to do His will! God may go through a lot of time and trouble to rock your world in order to help you make a decision for Him, but every man has a free will. Some Christians are so confused at times, that they feel they are doing God's will even when it is in direct disobedience to God's Word! How sad!

One last thing to keep in mind. YOU CAN'T **MAKE** SOMEONE LOVE YOU! People have the choice to love or not to love you. You can make the effort to try to win their hearts, but there is never any guarantee that their love will be yours. It is a CHOICE they must make. So please don't do what I did. I made foolish attempts to FORCE my departing spouse to love me. I felt so degraded when I would throw myself at the feet of my husband, who had already chosen to reject me, and have him reject me again, and again, and again. It doesn't work. You must concentrate on keeping peace with God in your own life. Do what God would have you to do in your situation, nothing less and nothing more. Keep your integrity and prevent further damage to your self-esteem.

CHAPTER 3
"LORD, I'M ANGRY!"

Divorce is one of the most stressful events that can happen in the life of a human being! According to the latest studies, the death of a spouse is the next most stressful event. However, there is usually no rejection of the spouse involved when a person leaves marriage by death.

I would sit by the phone and wait to see if God would answer my prayers by having my husband call me and say "Let's get back together!" I wanted so desperately to get my husband back, that I was to the point of calling him at work and trying to get a reassuring word from him that there was some hope of reconciliation. The desperate and lost feelings I felt drove me to be even more persistent in trying to win my husband's love back. I learned through experience, you cannot **MAKE** someone choose to love you. Loving someone is a choice! (Read the book, "Love is a Choice" by Hemfelt, Minirth Meier) You have a choice to continue loving someone or to stop loving them.

I remember feeling so guilty for being mad at my husband for divorcing me. I turned that anger inward, constantly searching for what I did wrong to deserve this kind of desertion. I honestly sought God to reveal the answer to me… and He did!

During One of my counseling sessions, I suddenly burst out crying to my counselor. I remember saying to him, "I'm so mad at my husband... I'm sorry, but I am so mad at him I feel I could really physically hurt him!" The words that came out of my counselor's mouth that day have stuck with me through all these years. I have used the same words over and over again to help others who have expressed these emotions in similar circumstances. He said, *"Lana, I'm glad you finally expressed your anger. It has to surface. If you don't allow it to surface, it will find other ways to surface which would be more damaging to you. It's O.K. to be angry. You have something to be angry about. Even God says in Ephesians 4:26 'Be angry but sin not.' Try to vent your anger in productive ways not destructive ways."* After my counselor spoke those words to me it was like a 1000-pound weight lifted from my shoulders. I had been carrying so much guilt for being angry about what my husband had done to me! Even God was angered at times but he did not sin in His anger (Exodus 32:10; Numbers 12:9; Psalm 95:11).

When we're in pain, we don't think very rationally. It takes someone with knowledge and experience to point us in the right direction. You can't help but be angry when you are hurt so badly by someone you love so much! The anger you feel when you are in pain is natural, although it doesn't give you a license to sin in your anger. If you are having difficulty in dealing with your anger or even acknowledging your anger, please read the book *"Make Anger Your Ally"* by Neil Clark Warren. I have read this book and it has helped with anger in a number of areas in my life. You must let your anger surface in order to deal with the situation, but it is possible to use it constructively, not destructively.

CHAPTER 4

MY LIFE WILL NEVER
BE THE SAME

What lay ahead in the days after that dread wintery day on my bedroom floor is what I really want to share with you. I prayed God would never let me forget the pain of divorce, loneliness, and frustration, especially as a woman who loved being married. I believe God has granted me that request for the sole purpose of sharing with others what God has done for me, and what I know He can do for you! I was single again - and starting over!

After the reality hit me that my husband was really leaving me, I phoned a pastor friend for counseling, and he referred me to a professional Christian counselor. Let me go on record as saying, I firmly believe in **solid Christian** counseling! I thank God for my counselor who God used to help me understand some of the emotions I was going through, and to learn to deal with them.

I loved being involved with the different ministries at church. I loved drama, evangelism, Sunday school, and many other places of ministry which I felt were now over! I was brought up in a denomination that had a strong doctrinal belief against granting ministerial credentials to anyone divorced and remarried. Needless to say, those who found themselves divorced within this denomination carried a stigma for the rest of their lives.

If I may, I would like to give you a word of advice if you find yourself under condemnation because you are a victim of divorce. PLEASE search the scriptures yourself and study what God has to say about divorce and remarriage. There are study aids to help you listed on the Recommended Reading page in the back of this book. Please be sure to take advantage of ALL the information available.

I had friends who had gone through divorce, and I watched as fellow believers held them at a distance in their friendships. I have learned that sometimes people just don't know how to respond to someone who is in a situation they don't understand. I remember feeling ostracized at times, even though there were many who tried to comfort and befriend me.

Whether it was because of the way I was brought up, or my own insecurities, I felt there was no place in ministry for me as a divorced woman. All I loved in serving God was over unless I remained single and believe me, I did not want to be single for the rest of my life! Why did I feel this way? Could it be because "divorcees" are a taboo among many Christians? Do others really look at you differently and sometimes actually treat you differently? Are divorcees different? Yes! I have become a different person from what I was before the divorce happened in my life! I have also come to the conclusion that it's O.K. to be different.

I thank God for raising up pastors and lay persons who feel the burden to work with divorced Christians. I believe the need for ministry to divorced persons is greater than it has ever been. I'm not sure the day will come again for families to be held together easily, especially considering what scripture has to say about the last days (Matthew 10:36).

I never wanted a divorce, and I didn't feel I did anything that warranted divorce. I was faithful to my husband and pure before the Lord in my relationship with Him. Why did I feel like God didn't want me anymore? Why did I feel like I was the one who failed in my marriage? In the heart of a Christian these are natural emotions.

There is never any harm in trying to improve yourself and trying to improve your relationships. But to blame yourself for the choices of your spouse is neither logical nor correct. The questions: "How could I have done better?" "Maybe I should have done something differently!" "Why didn't I...?" are natural responses. You are a normal human being!

Another word of advice: ponder these questions and get the best answers you can, then move on with your life! These are not the questions that will solve why your spouse dumped you! He chose to leave for his own reasons, and more than likely you will never be able to figure it all out. When people have a heart toward God and are faithful to their spouse, nothing will separate them! (Romans 8:35) However, when a person has a heart toward selfishness and sin, he will eventually fail God and his spouse (Mark 10:4-5).

Today, I can actually say I feel I am now a better person. A person whom God has tried and tested! I have learned to yield to Christ and allow Him to direct my life. I have come to understand some issues of life that others will **never** understand unless they have experienced an unwanted, Biblically unjust divorce. Did I enjoy divorce? Of course not! Would I want to go through it again? Of course not!

Today's society makes divorce easy for those who want out and difficult for those who are trying to keep their marriages together. The Court of Law would NOT let me REFUSE my husband's wishes for a divorce even though he had NO legal or Biblical reason to divorce me, except to follow his own desires. But, since I had no choice in the situation, I chose to

15

learn what I could from it. I asked God to turn the horrible nightmare of divorce into something that will make my life better than I've ever known before...and praise God...He did!

I DO NOT BELIEVE that everyone must go through a divorce in order to have the best that God has for them! God is able to work plan B when plan A is out of your control. For example. When Moses demanded that Pharaoh release the children of Israel and Pharaoh refused. How much easier it would have been to go with Plan A for Pharaoh - just let them go! But, since Plan A was not the choice of Pharaoh, God had to continue with Plan B (the plagues) until He completed His will in freeing His people. YOU ARE HIS PEOPLE!

If you will keep your trust in God and stay obedient to Him, he will take you through Plan B in order to complete the work and purpose He has begun in your life. There is nobody, or no thing that can separate you from the love of God. (Romans 8:35-39)

I am so thankful that God uses imperfect human vessels who are willing to be molded by Him! Gradually, I came to realize that God was not done working in my life, *"being confident of this, that He who began a good work in you will carry it on to completion."* Philippians 1:6. I believe God's Word is true and I had to believe He would complete what He wanted to do in my life, even though I had to face an ugly divorce.

I began praying for God to have His way in my life. I asked Him to take the pieces of my life I had left and use them for His glory! I also remember praying for the pain to go away. Looking back, I must tell you that time and perseverance are necessary ingredients for healing the wounded heart.

I speak now to you who are in the midst of the trial of divorce. PLEASE KNOW THAT GOD IS NOT DONE WITH YOUR LIFE! If I had pulled the trigger on that handgun in my bedroom during that wintery day, it would have been a great loss - for me! I would have missed out on some of the most beautiful times in my life!

When I was lying on that bedroom floor, crying my heart out to God to allow me to die, I would never have believed that God had some of the best times still in store for my life! No, my life would never be the same! God has restored to my life seven times the joy and happiness that was taken away through divorce!

I know God has a plan for your life, and if you will stay faithful to Him, He can take what looks like a hopeless situation and turn it into something that will make you into a better person and move you into realms that you never thought possible.

CHAPTER 5

HOW WILL I KNOW
WHEN TO LET GO?

I am a firm believer in doing everything you possibly can to keep your marriage together! In no way would I ever suggest to anyone that divorce is appropriate or the way out of a bad situation. God hates divorce...and so do I! However, when you are the victim of divorce and have no choice in what your spouse decides to do, you find yourself trying uselessly to fix what is broken!

I would like you to read a portion of a letter I wrote to a very close friend who was in the process of leaving her husband for her own reasons. Keep in mind that I wrote this letter a few years after my divorce and I could speak from first-hand experience:

"My Dear Sister in the Lord:

I am not aware of all the circumstances between you and your husband, and it's not often that I would get involved with someone else's private life, but God will not let me be at peace until I have shared my heart with you.

I love you dearly and always admired your sweet and gentle spirit. I appreciated YOU helping me when I was going through the trauma of divorce. I guess that's why I don't understand what's happening, but can only share what God has laid on my heart to say to you.

I know the pain of separation and divorce. It isn't easy on either person. I remember, as the party who didn't want divorce, feeling so rejected by my husband.

Sister, please understand that moving out of your home and marriage may seem like the answer to your problems, but you should know a few of the side effects according to professional counselors:

1. *Your moving out will always be viewed by your children and husband as a rejection of them. No matter what you say, it can't change their feelings.*

2. *90% of separations generally end up in a permanent separation or divorce. Please don't let anyone tell you otherwise!*

3. *When my husband left me, I knew it would have been very hard ever to trust him again even if he wanted to reconcile, which you know he never did.*

*Sister, **PLEASE TRY EVERYTHING YOU CAN TO WORK OUT YOUR MARRIAGE**! I know it must be a very trying situation that would make you want to leave the home, but give it all you've got!*

I still think holidays are the hardest on everybody. A time when there is supposed to be laughter, peace and joy is turned into endless episodes of where to spend the holiday and feelings of loneliness all over again. 70% of second marriages end in divorce because they are never able to blend the new family members together.

I love you and I know that I will always love you. Life will go on no matter what you both do, but one thing is sure...

we have no guarantees in life. I know the loneliness, fear, hardship, and yet, the treasure of a family. Please know you can call or write me anytime.

Please keep in touch, and if there is anything I can do, please let me know.

Jana

I love you

As you can see by this letter, I believe in making every effort to keep a marriage together. However, there does come a time when you know you have come to the end of all you can do in trying to keep your marriage together. God must be the one who gives you the permission and ability to let go of your marriage relationship.

Many victims of divorce are confused by what scripture gives as permission to let go of a departing spouse. I am not writing this book to give my view of the question on divorce and remarriage. However, I do **strongly** suggest you read the book "Divorce and Remarriage - Four Christian Views" by Carl Laney, William Heth, Thomas Edgar and Larry Richards. This book helps you see what scripture tells us about God's view of divorce and remarriage. Note: You MUST read the entire book!

A very good friend of mine was divorced by her husband for his secretary. The day the divorce was final he sent out invitations for his upcoming marriage to his secretary to take place in three weeks. I feel in this instance, she would have to ask God for the grace to begin letting go of her husband.

I counseled a middle-aged woman after church one evening who told me her husband left her for another woman eight years ago. Even though he kept promising to come back to her he always ended up leaving her for another woman. I couldn't tell this woman that hope was gone for that relationship, but I did suggest she read the book "Love Must Be Tough" by Dr.

James Dobson. She was subjecting herself to an emotional roller coaster for eight years with this man and either didn't want to let go of the relationship or couldn't let go.

There are instances when a person can hope and pray that a broken marriage will mend, and sometimes, Praise God, it does! God's Word tells us "WITH GOD ALL THINGS ARE POSSIBLE" and in conjunction with John 7:17 we understand that there is hope for troubled marriages for those who are willing. But it takes **willingness from BOTH parties involved** in order to accomplish the task of reconciliation!

You are responsible for your own life, actions and decisions. You cannot make your spouse decide to be a willing participant in reconciliation. It is his own choice! If your spouse chooses to disrupt the will of God flowing in his life and in your marriage relationship it does not need to disrupt God's will in your life! Scripture is VERY clear about allowing God to have His way in our lives. (Matthew 7:21)

Let God be the one to direct your heart in the area of "letting go." I would suggest reading the books listed in the back of this book to help you work through some of the difficulties of letting go.

Some good advice my counselor gave me when I was going through divorce:

1. Don't let your expectations get too high in looking for positive response from your spouse regarding reconciliation. When you expect him to react a certain way and he doesn't, you are disappointed and start an emotional downward trend.

2. When you try your best to keep your marriage together, and your spouse still wants out, you can lay your head on your pillow at night knowing you have done your best before God to keep your side of the

marriage vows. You will eventually sleep through the nights...! promise you!

3. Give yourself time to heal before you make any major decisions in your life. Sometimes you just want to get away and move to the other side of the world. Wait! Let God help you work through the pain, and eventually you will know what direction you want to take with your life. I would suggest waiting at least one or two years, if possible, before making any major decisions.

After I accepted the fact that my husband wasn't coming back to me, I knew I had to get the mind set of getting on with my life. Easier said than done. But God was with me each step of the way!

I started to read a lot of books on relationships and divorce which helped prepare me for some of the emotions I would be going through in the months and even years to come. I knew when it was time for me to let go of the "hoped for" reconciliation between me and my former husband. I think the hardest part of letting go for me was not knowing what would happen to me without this loved one in my life. I knew God wanted me to get on with what He had for my life and believe me...MY LIFE WOULD NEVER BE THE SAME!

CHAPTER 6
I DON'T WANT TO START OVER!

*I*f you have children living at home or even own a pet, I guess it helps ease the loneliness of the night. However, since I had neither, and was determined to begin life again, I figured the first step to re-establishing my life would be learning to live alone. Some people may like that idea, but I never did.

I was very grateful for my precious mother and family who made me feel so welcome while I lived with mom. But I wanted a place of my own again. I sometimes felt like a vagabond roaming from place to place until I finally had enough money and nerve to begin again. I lived with my mom for about eight months after the divorce. Not only did my Mom give me moral support, but living with her for those few months helped me financially until I was able to afford a simple condominium.

Since I very rarely spent nights alone in my entire life, it was a very strange feeling for me when I had to move out on my own again - all alone.

I knew there would be very little maintenance if I chose to live in a condominium. Also, all the outdoor work (lawns, snow removal, building repair, etc.) would be taken care of by the condominium association. So, I bought myself a humble condominium and began living on a tight budget!

I do remember one of my first frustrations of being a woman living alone. I guess it would be like a man who had never cooked or cleaned house attempting to cook a gourmet meal and iron his own shirts.

I needed to change a light bulb outside on my porch. I decided I could do it myself. Ha! All I had to do was get the cover off the light fixture, right? The insecurity of having to begin life over, even though I didn't want to, and feeling incompetent to change a little light bulb began a flood of tears streaming down my cheeks as I was on the ladder! The more I tried to get that "intricate" light fixture off to change the bulb, the more I cried. I was very angry at my ex-husband for doing this to me!

I found out, in the months to come, that those feelings would return whenever I had to venture into areas that reminded me that I had to begin life all over again. It really wasn't the light bulb at all. It was my feeling of helplessness not having had a choice to say, "I don't want to start over!"

If you want to begin enjoying life again, you must know that starting over is not bad. I thank God for His faithfulness to me and to all those who trust in Him. During the years I spent alone I saw the Lord work on my behalf over and over again. He taught me that starting over was just another way of learning and growing as a human being. I wouldn't trade those special times I saw God intervene and provide for the needs in my life for anything in the world. It was exciting to see how God displayed His love and faithfulness to me!

He undertook in my finances in ways that I'd never thought of. It seemed the Lord would have someone to help me in every situation which gave me much difficulty.

When my emotions finally stabilized after the divorce, I went back to work in a secular workplace. It really wasn't my heart's desire to work in an office supply store, but I was thankful for the income. Beggars can't be choosers, they say. But when scripture says "My God shall meet all your needs according to His riches in Glory." (Phil 4:19), I think God means it!

I began to pray each day that God would give me a job in a Christian atmosphere. Two months later, I began being harassed by an employee at the office supply store. It became so bad that I felt I had to find another job. I felt God telling me to quit my job and He would supply the next one. You must understand, it was very out of character for me to quit one job without having another one lined up! I had a tight budget!

This is one of those fun times when you wish God would just write you a note and let you know what He's doing. But, I gave my two weeks notice and never told anybody I knew that I didn't have another job lined up. I guess I felt everyone would think it was a pretty stupid move.

I finished my last day on a Friday. When I was in church the following Sunday, an acquaintance approached me about working for him as a secretary. It just happened that he was a state executive for the church denomination I attended and the job would be in a totally Christian environment! Wow!

When he asked me if I was looking for a job, I became so anxious, that I told him I would pray about it so I wouldn't appear too eager! I knew I didn't need to pray about it, but I told him I would let him know in a few days.

God knew I would need to start that job in two days when they called me back and asked me to come in as soon as possible. God has perfect timing, and He blessed me with an opportunity working for people that I loved and still love.

After my divorce, I had many friends and acquaintances who took part in helping me. I wasn't accustomed to letting people help me. Instead of helping them, I had to learn to let them help me.

I remember a special friend who was such a blessing to me when my finances were especially low. He repaired things in my home that would have cost me a lot of money to have repaired any other way.

Eventually, I was blessed with a special friend who also became my housemate. Her payment of rent really helped contribute financially to my monthly mortgage payment.

God will bring people into your life whom you need to help get you through. I was so used to helping others that it was difficult for me to learn how to accept kindness from them.

I know God has a balance when it comes to the laws of giving and receiving. Allow God to bless your life. When you are faithful to pay your tithes and give God back what He has given you, He will honor His Word (Malachi 3:10). One of the promises of God is, "If we sow, we shall also reap" (II Cor. 9:6).

One of the best things you can do during your time of recovery from divorce is not only to pay your tithes, but to help others any way you can. It serves as a therapy for your own healing and you will always reap the benefits of sowing "good seed" in one way or another.

Don't be afraid to try and learn new things and develop new skills: ladies, like changing light bulbs, men, like starching and ironing that dress shirt! God is going to be by your side if you will let Him! So, let Him!

CHAPTER 7

SINGLE AGAIN! NOT BY CHOICE!

Well, there I was, Friday night, nowhere to go, no one to go there with, and not sure if I really wanted to go anywhere anyway! Especially a "singles' meeting"! Family and friends were so gracious in urging me to get involved socially. Again, easier said than done!

Where did I fit in now? I was no longer the "other half" of a couple. I was too young to be involved with the senior citizens brigade, too old to run with the wild youth group, and I really didn't feel like a "single"!

Sure, there was a Valentine Banquet, but I no longer had a Valentine to take me, and I knew I would feel like a fifth wheel if I attended that gala. There was the high school basketball game for teens and their parents, but I wasn't a parent and I surely was not a teenager. I guess I could have gone to Bill Knapp's with the senior citizens brigade, but I felt that might be pushing it a little and I surely didn't FEEL like a single to attend any singles parties...so, where did I fit in? What about those who have just gone through the trauma of divorce?

I happened to be one of the fortunate few who attended a church that sponsored a Singles Group Ministry. I had mixed emotions about ever attending any singles events. I felt if I attended singles events it would be a sure sign to everyone else that I was different. I just knew when I arrived at the singles meeting that night they would surely pin a sign on my lapel saying, "Available." I had an awful lot to learn about being single again. I had to learn that the times of fellowship I had with other singles could be just as gratifying as my times with couples when I was married.

So, Friday night came, and it was time for Singles Friday Volleyball. I literally went out the door as frightened as a child, not sure what to expect on the first day of kindergarten! What would I say to people when I arrived there? Would I know anybody there? What were they like? Would they like me? It didn't take long for me to realize that my feelings were just feelings of "starting over."

I went to my first Singles Meeting that Friday night and actually, enjoyed it so much I went back again. And again. And again. I eventually became a singles leader at our church and began helping plan the events for the Singles Group and studying how to minister to their needs.

I now realize how vital it is to have ministry groups available for singles and how important it is for singles to get involved in some kind of ministry. If your church does not have a Singles' Ministry, I challenge you to pray and ask God to use you to start one (with your Pastor's permission of course!). I guarantee that there will always be people who will need this kind of ministry in your church.

On Valentine's Day the following year, instead of feeling like a fifth wheel at a couple's banquet (unless you had a date to attend with you) we had a Singles Party of our own...it was great! It is good to schedule events for single parents and their children as well.

Divorced or never married or widowed (old or young), in order to have a balanced life you must take some time out to socialize. You need to be determined to make friends who have the common thread of being single. By no means am I suggesting you give up your friendships with couples or others. Singles still need to be involved in their church as a whole. It's healthy, both emotionally and spiritually, to have ALL the family of God be a part of fellowship.

At times, I sensed that some of my lady friends felt as though I had now become a threat to their marriages just because I was single. I could see a hesitation about forming a close friendship in some circumstances, which I have now come to understand.

Some marriages are threatened easily when a man or woman who used to be married is now single and learning to be happy as a single. This may tend to threaten some married people who are NOT happy in their marriages. These people are easily threatened anyway because of their insecurity and unhappiness. They may view your happiness as encouraging their spouses to wish to be single. Or they may themselves desire to be single again, yearning secretly to be out of their marriage. This has NOTHING TO DO WITH YOUR BEING SINGLE!

Some people are not threatened by an "unhappy" single but will be threatened by a "happy" single. I suggest that you be careful and be sensitive to those who don't understand, or have insecurities in their marriages that may cause them to treat you as if you had the "plague." Time will help to overcome the "stigma" placed on singles. I believe it is God's will for anyone who is a Christian to be happy...whether single or married!

Another type of "friend" you may want to prepare yourself for is those who don't understand, and probably don't want to understand, your situation. The Lord helped me to realize that people really don't understand the pain of divorce and may never understand unless they find themselves in the same situation.

People don't like dealing with issues they don't understand. And believe me, you will have many people trying to analyze who did what wrong, and whose fault it really was for the divorce. I had "friends" who came to me while I was going through some of the toughest days of my life and suggest what I should have done to save my marriage, or what I shouldn't have done that destroyed my marriage.

When you are falsely accused at a time like that in your life, you either feel like crying or like tearing heads off because your accusers don't know what they are talking about! Understand this...they just don't understand. I remember hearing several different reasons from other people concerning why my marriage had failed, none of which were correct. You will have to pray for God's grace to forgive what they say to you or about your divorce situation. GOD KNOWS THE TRUTH and it's not necessary to defend the truth, just to speak it!

You will be hard pressed to try and set everyone straight about what went on in your marriage that led to divorce. Don't feel that you MUST tell people about your private life. This is why I suggest having one or two very close friends, of your own sex, to confide in and talk to from your heart.

Christian singles are a unique breed. They love Christ, so they don't wish to participate in "bar hopping," immorality, living with someone, or anything else that would grieve the heart of our precious, loving God in heaven. This limits the kind of friends they have and the types of places they can go. Be creative...there are always places like the zoo, picnics, state parks, sports, plays, concerts, unique restaurants, group trips and so much more!

I made many friends whom I will always consider to be my friends whether they get married or stay single. I wouldn't trade the days of making these new friends for anything! They are good friends because we can relate to one another and fellowship comfortably together. Try to be friends with everyone, but have a few close trustworthy friends with whom you can pray and share your innermost feelings. It will be so beneficial to your emotional healing.

You will have many opportunities to make new friends and try new adventures. You will make friends that will last for a lifetime!

CHAPTER 8

A NEW DIRECTION

One wintery, snowy day I was driving to the shopping mall and was trying to find a parking space close to the main door. It was the busy Christmas season and the mall was very crowded.

I was in an area of shopping where most ladies would not feel comfortable being alone. But I didn't feel afraid as much as I was hoping to have a shorter walk to the mall entrance. I whispered a prayer and asked God to help me with this silly request of getting a parking spot near the door. Just a split second after I finished whispering this prayer I started to turn my car toward the back of the parking lot. As I began to do so, God immediately spoke to me and said "What are you doing?" I said, "Lord, I'm looking for a parking space!" He said, "Didn't you just ask me to help you find a space near the door?" "Yes," I said. "Then why are you heading for the back of the lot? Why don't you go in the direction you asked me for?

I began sobbing in the middle of the parking lot as I headed toward the front and found an open spot just two spaces away from the main entrance! I wasn't crying just because God gave me this beautiful parking spot. I was crying because I knew that the Lord was talking to me about more than just where I drove my car. He was dealing with me about my life!

I sat in my car and bawled at all the scriptures of promise He brought to my mind during those trying days of divorce (Psalm 91; Isaiah 49:2; Isaiah 51:16). I felt the Lord speak to my heart and say, "Stay obedient and I will do it!"

How many times do we ask God to move on our behalf and then act as though He never heard us? God was showing me that I must move in the direction that He had given me!

When God decides to do something in our lives, nothing can stand in His way except us! Not even an unfaithful spouse. God works beyond any man-made barriers and does what He does best: proving what man thinks is impossible, God makes possible! (Matthew 19:26) God uses those who are pure and yielded before Him in ways beyond our imagination.

I tried to be as obedient as I knew how in every aspect of my life. I began to pray that God would have His will in any future relationships. Again, I must thank my Spirit-filled counselor, who gave me some of the best advice in my life about future relationships. I know beyond a shadow of a doubt that Satan would have enjoyed destroying any chance of my having a happy future. He knows all the tactics to use. Like making you think you are ready for a relationship just weeks or even months after you have gone through the divorce.

Believe me, there are plenty of men and women out in our world today who would like to take advantage of your vulnerability during the first year or two after your divorce. If God has given you a release in your spirit to get on with your life and you know there is NO CHANCE of reconciliation with your ex-spouse, PLEASE go slowly in developing any relationships with the opposite sex. I thank God for keeping His hand in my life.

I remember thinking how ready I was to go on my first outing with someone of the opposite sex...all by ourselves! It felt so nice to have the compliments and attention that I had been deprived of for so long. Just a simple "You look great" made me feel like a million bucks! But PLEASE BEWARE! You need to step back and allow yourself to see that person without all those compliments and "goo-gooing" over you. Your emotions have not leveled out yet if you are sponging up every little positive word you receive from someone and feel like you are suddenly falling in love!

Is he respecting your on-going recovery from a divorce? Or pushing you to develop a closer relationship with him? Chances are if someone really cares about you, he will allow you a good amount of space to recover emotionally from the mega-hit on your self-esteem.

Also remember, since you already have been married, you know what you are missing sexually by being a single Christian. You need to pray and ask God to help you to stay pure for the person whom God may ultimately have for you! It's harder to move slowly in a serious relationship when you are more knowledgeable about the opposite sex. Don't let Satan fool you into thinking you will grow old without ever experiencing the joy of being intimate again with someone you dearly love. Satan WILL try to deceive you! Be aware of his devices (Ephesians 6:10-18 ; II Cor 2:11) as God instructs us.

Try to remember that God is going to take you in a new direction in life. This doesn't mean that it is a "second rate" way of life...it means a NEW and DIFFERENT way of living for you.

CHAPTER 9

NEW FRIENDS AND A NEW LIFE

*A*fter I finally got through the hardest part of my divorce recovery, I realized that I really could enjoy my life the way it was...being single again! I would never have chosen this route for my life but my ex-spouse gave God no alternative. GOD BLESSED ME BEYOND MY EXPECTATIONS! He gave me a new life and new friends!

When I began to pray about future relationships and friends in my life, I knew I wouldn't be ready for any relationships with the opposite sex for quite a while. This gave me needed time to draw closer to God and know that I could be happy as a single, too. The harder the the trial the closer we draw toward God and this was exactly what happened in my life. I was 35 years old and had been a Christian for 26 years when divorce struck my life. But I had never known a relationship with God the way I came to know Him then. It still boggles my mind to think of how much God cared for me in my time of need.

I remember God giving me dreams that left me with such a peace that when I woke in the morning, I felt His presence all over the room. One night, I particularly remember, God gave me a dream of my in-filling of His precious Holy Spirit. I remember crying and yet feeling such a presence of God in that dream that when I finally awoke, I had a peace that never left me for the rest of my lonely nights. Nights that I endured trying to fall asleep to Christian radio until 3:00 AM vanished, and I could sleep like a baby! What a wonderful God we serve!

I kept holding onto the scripture from Ephesians that claimed "All things work together for good to them that love the Lord and are called according to His purpose." I didn't understand how God could take the pieces of my life and put them together, but somehow God gave me the ability to hold on to His promise. And God did it!

It was over two years later that God brought me a wonderful and beautiful blessing. A new friend entered my life whom God would use to change my future forever, Steven Arthur Bach. He, too, had gone through the difficult pain of divorce. He was a minister and had a wholly different set of issues to deal with when his wife of 22 years left him for another man.

I really became acquainted with Steve when I discovered he had just gone through a tragic divorce. I simply wanted to be a friend to him by letting him know exactly what I am telling you in this book. I tried to reassure him that God will continue to use him in ministry and nobody or nothing can stop God from having His way in his life, unless he chose to stop God.

Steve and I became friends and enjoyed each other's company before we ever entertained the thought of dating. I must give credit where credit is due. It all began when the office of friends I worked with decided to have a company bar-b-que at Steve's home. The day before the bar-b-que everybody but myself and another gal announced they couldn't make it. Whether it was planned or God choreographed it, my girl friend and I ended up going to play miniature golf with Steve rather than have a bar-b-que for just three people.

Of course, I surprised Steve with my unique putting skills and shortly after the game our girlfriend said she had to get home. This left Steve and me in a McDonald's having coffee for almost four hours. We discussed our entire lives on that night. Little did we know that God was bringing our lives together and He had a plan for our lives far better than what we could ever have imagined.

Steve ended up phoning me later that week to ask me out for dinner. Of course, I obliged...and obliged...and obliged. Thus began a period of courtship, which led to engagement, which led to a beautiful wedding where Steve and I exchanged marriage vows with new God-given hearts filled with love, dedication, and anticipation of what God would do in our lives.

I never knew God could restore my happiness a hundred fold! But I do now! The Lord has placed Steve and me into a ministry that both of us are thankful to be used in for His Glory.

I am not telling you about this wonderful man and new life that God gave me just to tell you how happy I am! I want to share with you that God is still working in your life at this very moment! God never abandons those who desire His presence in their lives and are trying to serve Him! ("Come near to God and He will come near to you" James 4:8).

In all circumstances, God is still God. You MUST believe that He has everything under control. If you yield your life to Him, He will begin a new work in you. One day you will look back and say, "Thank you God! You brought me through!"

CHAPTER 10

GOD IS NOT FINISHED
WITH YOUR LIFE!

I recently learned that a girlfriend of mine was experiencing this devastating tragedy called divorce. She was a beautiful, talented, godly young lady. As newlyweds, her spouse, who claimed to be a Christian, began abusing her and eventually broke his vows to her and to God, leaving her devastated and angry at God. She felt that He could have prevented this event by just warning her not to marry this man. She felt that God must not be a big enough God if He couldn't change the one person she loved most and cause her marriage to be a success. God burdened me to write her this letter. I would like to share just a portion of this letter with you. I have changed the names for the sake of confidentiality.

"Susan, I too had a hard time coming to grips with why God allowed my spouse to leave me. I went through eight months of professional Christian counseling and it all boiled down to this one truth: each person has a will of his own. And because we are ALL constantly changing, we have a choice in which direction our lives go...either toward righteousness or away from God's righteousness. No matter what anybody says or does...including our fervent praying...IF THAT PERSON IS SO DETERMINED TO GO HIS OWN WAY, HE

*WILL GO!, GOD WILL NOT **MAKE** SOMEONE CHOOSE RIGHTEOUSNESS! God can create circumstances in order for that person to see the error of his way, but it is still the choice of each individual as to how they live!*

God never promised us that we would be untouched by other people's sins...in fact that is the hardest part of living. We are always affected by each other's sin.

Susan, YOU are SPECIAL to God! And believe me, God still has a plan for your life. God is still God! I want to share a few scriptures with you that the Lord gave me during the days that I truly doubted Him:

***Isaiah 40:28-31** The Lord gave me this scripture to let me know that He was with me through it all.*

***Job 42:10-17** When I was mad at God and doubted that He knew what was going on in my life and thought He could never fix it!*

***Isaiah 43:18-19** He gave me these words as a promise that He can do a NEW work in my (and your) life! Amen!*

I love you, Susan! I told your mom that I still feel God has a special work for you! We love you, Susan. Most of all, God loves you! He's not finished with you yet!"

Your friend,

At the lowest time in my life, God was still God. He doesn't change because we are going through hard trials. We change, hopefully for the good, toward God. Keep a tender heart toward God and watch what He will do with your life.

I thank God for my family and Christian friends who stuck by me and supported me with their prayers and love through my whole ordeal. God used each one to be a help to me! My mom, dad, brothers, sister, aunts, nieces, nephews, everybody cared so much about me. Some of my Christian friends, though I was selective in who I confided in, were caring and there were especially some pastor friends who were very helpful during this time.

I know finances can be a big problem when starting over. I know making new friends is difficult, explaining the situation to children is hard, dealing with Christian friends who are misinformed can be disappointing, but you can be an overcomer. Surround yourself with God's Word and His people who will support you with prayer and love.

Forget the old life but learn from your mistakes. There will always be scars that you will carry in your heart, but they are proof of a battle, and you won the battle! Allow God to use His healing balm on your heart. Time is an important factor in the healing of any emotional trauma.

Loving is a risk you must take. Love will always have some pain along the way. Just because you stub your toe on the sidewalk, do you stop walking? No, you give it time to heal and are more careful walking on that sidewalk the next time. It's the same with our lives. As Zig Ziglar (author of many "succeeding in life" books) always says "Failure is not a person, it's an event." Be gentle on yourself and be willing to adventure into your new frontier. God loves you and has great things in store for your life. You must make the effort to find out what they are! "Trust God and lean not unto your own understanding, acknowledge Him in all your ways and He shall direct your paths (Proverbs 3:5-6)."

CHAPTER 11

A WORD TO THOSE NOW
EXPERIENCING DIVORCE RECOVERY

I remember hearing a song on the radio about a middle-aged man who, not by choice, was single again. The song spoke about getting ready for his first date and how awkward he felt! Let's face it...it is awkward! I know God gave permission in special circumstances to re-marry (I Corinthians 7-15; Matthew 19:9). But what you must go through in order to be sure you want to remarry is no party!

1. Pray, Pray, Pray & Pray

You know the importance of prayer. It is a must! Some of the best prayer times I ever had in my life were when I was single and seeking God's will for my life. God is there waiting to commune with you. Allow Him to be your best friend now and for the rest of your life!

2. Read, Read, Read & Read Some More

PLEASE read the many books on relationships in Christian bookstores. You will find a list of the ones I recommend in the back of this book. They helped me tremendously and I know they will help you too!

3. Don't be a rebound.

Don't allow someone else to use you as a rebound relationship. PLEASE don't fall into a situation where you feel you have found your true love one month after your search has begun. Friendships take time and you MUST realize your vulnerability.

4. Prepare yourself for future relationships.

If this means receiving Christian counseling, then please do so! It is very important that you know when you are ready to embark on a new relationship. Sometimes there are issues we must deal with that we don't even know exist. For example: I remember having absolute distrust for men for quite a while after my divorce. I had to deal with distrust of men and the fear that they would hurt me by deserting me again. My counselor helped me immensely in this area and I was able to recognize its ugly head when it came up in some of my starting relationships.

5. Be sure to look for someone who is not like the last one.

Counselors will often warn people who have been in a relationship of abuse or desertion to be careful that they aren't drawn to the same kind of person. Sometimes you are unaware of why you are drawn to certain types of personalities. There is a book that will help you by Alfred Ellis entitled "One-Way Relationships - When You Love Them More Than They Love You." You must make an effort to seek books and/or counseling on how to choose a mate right for you. Remember, you are a different person through all this, and you now have experience to help you improve your choices. Make the right one.

I made a list before the Lord of the traits I desired in a mate for the rest of my life. I literally prayed over this list and sought God for His will in the mate He had for me. It's easy to think that God has overlooked you when He is passing out mates but trust me, He hasn't forgotten you. Be patient and don't settle for "second" best in your life!

6. Try not to project old memories and fears on your new mate.

I told myself that I would never give my heart to any man again. I was sure he would hurt me and desert me. It's easy to transfer our fears to someone who has absolutely not caused them! CAUTION: This is why you must be sure you pray for a personality good for you. Dating someone who has had three divorces because of unfaithfulness would NOT be a good choice for you. You would have a hard time trusting him and at the same time healed wounds may be opened up all over again.

Try to rid yourself of the excess baggage that comes as a result of being rejected through divorce. Feelings of insecurity, low self-esteem, distrust, anger, and so many other emotions can tend to cling on for quite a while.

It is necessary to allow these feelings to surface, and yet after having dealt with them properly, allow God to heal you. Help Him out by not holding on to them! My new God-given husband, Steven, has an excellent ministry video titled "The Poison of a Bitter Spirit." You can watch this video on our ministry website at: www.LanaBach.com. It will help you understand how you can let go of some of those ill feelings.

7. Consider the cost before remarrying, especially when children are involved.

Again, let me say that loving is a risk! Today's statistics show that over 50% of all marriages in America today fail in divorce. They also tell us that 75% of all second marriages fail in divorce. I don't want to sound pessimistic, but I do want you to be aware and careful in selecting a new mate.

The four primary causes of most divorces are the following:

1. Money

2. Children

3. Sex

4. In-Laws

Mates will be unable to agree on one or more of these.

Please know that blending families together in a second marriage can be VERY difficult. A daughter doesn't want to accept her new stepmother, a stepson feels the favoritism of his stepfather to his real son, and on and on it can go. There is a reason why so many second marriages end in divorce. Please step back from any situation you are contemplating getting involved in, and be sure you are willing to take the hard along with the easy!

My advice would be that both families seek Christian counseling BEFORE marriage. A lot of issues can be avoided before they ever come up.

I love being married, yet every marriage is going to have rough spots. Learn to work on issues rather than avoid them or pretend they don't exist. God will help you as you BOTH seek His guidance for your families.

There are three ingredients a relationship must have to build a strong marriage, trust, respect, and love. Make sure you hold up your part of the relationship in these areas. In healthy relationships, trust will breed trust, respect will breed respect and love will breed love. Enjoy the benefits of a healthy relationship!

Just a few more notes to those of you who are experiencing the pain of divorce at this very moment:

There is something my mother told me before I ever heard it anywhere else and that is, "Helping others will help you."

How true! When you begin to reach out to others even though you yourself are hurting, somehow your own pain seems to lessen.

The value of our lives is determined by how much we give to others (Matthew 10:39). Find ways to help others and you will be surprised how much better you will feel. Your needs seem to diminish amidst the action of your caring for others.

Don't be too hard on yourself as you are recovering from this devastation. Learn to laugh at yourself and just learn to laugh period! The Bible tells us that "Laughter is like medicine to the soul" Proverbs 17:22.

CHAPTER 12

SURVIVING THE FINANCIAL
DEVASTATION OF DIVORCE

I know finances can be a big problem when starting your life over. My advice would be to create a budget. During my divorce recovery period I remember having a budget that consisted of $3.00 per day in gasoline for my car and $10 a week for entertainment. Needless to say, I CUT, CUT, CUT any luxuries!

In creating a financial budget, you MUST determine what has priority in order for you to keep up with your financial obligations. There are many books available in the Christian bookstores on how to set up a budget for your household. I suggest you make a wise investment in one of those books and start a budget immediately.

My father gave me a lot of good advice on finances throughout the years and I want to pass on some of his advice to you along with some Biblical advice:

1. Tithe

The Bible is very clear about tithing and giving back to God what belongs to Him. Not tithing would be actually robbing God. However, since we are under grace rather than law, a tenth is the very least we should give to God. What you give over and above the tenth is real giving. When you put God first in your finances you will find it easier to put Him first in other areas of your life as well. You also allow God the privilege of blessing your life and your finances (Luke 6:38).

2. Savings

Just as you set aside ten percent for God you must set aside another ten percent toward savings. It is vitally important to force yourself to save, otherwise you will never be able to plan for the future and care for emergencies.

3. Housing

I know it was difficult for me to move in with my mom after my divorce, as much as I love her, because I was so accustomed to living in my own home. Just remember that some circumstances are temporary as you get back on your feet again. I am so thankful that I had family there to help me during this difficult time.

One thing you should definitely try to do is to get back on your own and possibly find a roommate (of the same sex of course!) to move in and share expenses with you.

4. Food

Your health is important. You may want to create a budget for your food expense and stick to it! Eating at home will be the most cost-efficient way to have your meals. I used to budget myself a few times a week to eat out with friends. In the meantime, having a food budget affords you the opportunity to be a really good cook! Start saving coupons!

5. Automobile

Owning and operating a car is going to be a definite expense, and a high one at that. You have payments, repair, gas, insurance, maintenance, etc. It is always nice to have this amenity but also consider taking public transportation until you are back on your feet again.

Sometimes it's possible to share rides to work and alternate drivers each week as each person puts in for gas. This would help cut the cost down of driving each day.

6. Health Insurance

One thing you cannot afford to let go is your health insurance! You may not enjoy making the premium payments if you are healthy, but if you get sick you will really be happy you have the insurance.

Most employers offer some type of plan you can be a part of, and it would be my advice to you to seek the best plan for you and your family.

7. Life Insurance

If you were to die tomorrow, who would pay for your funeral expense? It would be disastrous to think that your family would need to go into debt for your funeral. Please seek a policy that would at least cover funeral expenses. As you get back on your feet you may wish to consider increasing your insurance for the sake of your children, if you have any.

8. Credit Cards

Credit cards can get you into some big trouble if you are not disciplined to pay them off each month. My advice would be to stay away from credit cards for the time being.

Also, becoming an expert garage sale shopper can help you save on items like furniture and other household items. Some of my furniture that I love the most I found at an estate sale. If you aren't sure of what quality you're buying, then take someone along who can help you look at what you need. You will save money, guaranteed!

Turn a hobby into a money maker! You may have some talent of needlework, woodworking, or some other type of hobby that you can use to earn extra income. You may be able to sell to personal friends or have items sold on consignment at a local store. Try it!

One last suggestion about finances: "LIVE BELOW YOUR MEANS." If you are constantly living from paycheck to paycheck and scraping the bottom each week you won't have a very secure feeling. There is a sense of freedom when you know you could allow yourself to spend more.

Allow the extra money for traveling, maybe music lessons or something you want to reward yourself with for being so frugal with your finances. One of the ways God provides for us is giving us the common sense to know how to manage our money. Those who are living from paycheck to paycheck find themselves worrying about what they will wear, eat, etc.

Put God first in your finances and ask Him for wisdom in your expenditures. I often still ask the Lord to direct my spending. It's a great way to reduce frivolous spending!

CHAPTER 13

EFFECTS OF DIVORCE
ON FAMILY MEMBERS

*T*he aftermath of divorce on family members is like the waves created by a stone thrown into a calm pond. There will be many lives affected, especially those children who have witnessed the harsh blow of divorce on the parents whom they love so much.

There are parents and in-laws who want to have their "turn" at getting to that spouse who hurt their loved one so deeply. Sometimes they would not want to see their loved one ever reconciled with that spouse, even if it were possible!

You must expect that there will be side effects of divorce on each family member but there are some suggestions that I can make to help ease some of that tension and pain.

I remember having to defend myself each time a family member asked what I would do if "so and so" wanted to reconcile. At certain times it seemed that they had a rougher time dealing with my situation than I did. I had to reassure them that I was seeking counsel and being cautious in each step.

I now understand that my family didn't want to see me hurt again, by getting back with the former spouse without seeing any repentance on his part. They wanted to hear that I was aware of his poor behavior (not excusing it) and that my pain would not drive me back to him unless there was genuine repentance.

Of course, I never had the opportunity to be reconciled with my former spouse and that dispelled a lot of the anxiety my family was going through. Remember that your family is hurting for you and they don't want to see you hurt again by the same person or any other person who comes into your life.

If you have any future hope of being reconciled with your spouse it would be wise NOT to expose every little detail to your family members of how badly he treated you during your marriage and divorce.

I suggest you find a close personal friend or counselor to listen as you air out your emotions during this difficult time rather than allowing your family members to hear the heart wrenching details of how your spouse may have wrongfully treated you. I discovered that once I was back on track in life, it was actually easier for me to deal with the emotions of that pain than it was for my family.

Another important suggestion that I feel will help you is that you be careful not to let your children hear you "bad mouthing" their other parent! As much as he has put you through, you must, for your children's sake, express the importance of loving that parent to your children.

Coming from a divorced home, I can honestly say that neither my mom, nor my dad ever tried to make any of us children hate the other parent. In fact, they both strived to help us learn to love the other parent despite their divorce. This helped reassure me of the love that each of my parents still had for me as I was growing up. This concept may be hard for some of you to follow or grasp but believe me, IT IS IMPORTANT!

I advise you to read the books recommended on this topic and those listed in the back of this book to help you know how to deal with issues that always come up with children of divorced parents.

There are no winners when it comes to divorce. Everybody loses. Children, family members, friends, and even our pets become damaged and broken!

This may seem silly, but I cried my eyes out when I had to let my beautiful dog, a yellow lab retriever, go live with my ex-husband because I could not have pets where I lived after the divorce. Even though I knew I could always get another dog, I loved that dog! A number of months later, I discovered that my dog had to be put to sleep because he had cancer. I really feel my dog had gone through trauma triggered by our separation.

The only redemption there is in any divorce situation is knowing Jesus Christ as your Savior and allowing Him to turn your life back into more than being a winner. He can turn your life from being a victim to being a victorious person!

YOU ARE NOT ALONE! God has brought many people through the same fiery trial which you are now experiencing.

As Job said, **"But, God knows the way that I take; when he has tested me, I will come forth as gold."** Job 23:10

You can make it! God's not done with your life! You are becoming a better person as you stay faithful to God. When this trial passes your life can be a shining testimony to your family, friends and the world around you of God's keeping power through the most painful of life's trials.

God bless and keep you, my friend, He did me!

I strongly want to urge every reader of this book to make Jesus Christ your personal Savior and Lord. If you, my friend, have not done this in your life, please pray this prayer of faith and confession with me:

Dear God, I confess to you my need of forgiveness. I ask you to forgive me of my sins. I acknowledge that I have sinned and have failed you. Thank you for sending Jesus Christ, your son, to die on the cross for me, and saving me from eternal death.

I ask Jesus to come into my heart and cleanse me from all sin. I ask you, Jesus, to be Lord of my life. I will confess my devotion and love for you to others. From this day forward, I will make Jesus Christ the Lord and Savior of my life. I will honor God, and live for Him every day for the rest of my life. I pray this in the name of Jesus Christ – MY SAVIOR AND LORD! Amen

If you would like to more information and material regarding your new life in Christ, please feel free to contact our Encouragement Ministries office at: www.LanaBach.com

PO Box 510

Stanwood, Michigan

49346

RECOMMENDED READING LIST

Building Your Mates Self-Esteem by Dennis & Barb Rainey
(Here '5 Life Publishers)

Growing Through Divorce by Jim Smoke
(Harvest House Publishers)

Imperative People by Dr. Les Carter
(Thomas Nelson Publishers)

Lonely Husbands, Lonely Wives by Dennis Rainey
(Word Publishers)

Love is a Choice by Dr. Robert Hemfelt, Dr. Frank Minirth,
Dr. Paul Meier (Thomas Nelson Publishers)

Love Must Be Tough by Dr. James C. Dobson
(Word Publishers)

**One Way Relationships - When You Love Them More
Than They Love You** by Alfred Ells
(Thomas Nelson Publishers)

Pursuit of Intimacy by David & Terese Ferguson and Chris
& Holly Thurman (Thomas Nelson Publishers)

Straight Talk by Dr. James C. Dobson
(Word Publishers)

The Lies We Believe by Dr. Chris Thurman
(Thomas Nelson Publishers)

Unmasking the Myths of Marriage by Ken Abraham
(Published by Fleming H. Revell Company)

ABOUT ENCOURAGEMENT MINISTRIES, INC.

*M*any people are hurting! They have been scarred and wounded by unkind realities in life. God desires to bring a special word of comfort to soothe the sorrowing soul. This is the focus of Encouragement Ministries, Inc.

Lana was married to Rev. Steven Bach, Founder of Encouragement Ministries, Inc. for almost 30 years before the Lord called him home in 2022. Having personally walked through the heartbreak of losing a soulmate, and her years of experience in ministry with Steve, have uniquely qualified her to speak to a variety of life's painful circumstances.

As a speaker and teacher, Lana passionately shares how the healing power of God can transform even the most difficult circumstances from pain into purpose.

Whether invited to share her personal story, speak at church, or teach at a ministry conference, Lana will challenge the audience to go deeper in Christ.

For more information on Lana's ministry please go to: www. LanaBach.com

A PERSONAL NOTE FROM LANA

I wrote this book in 1997 and since then there has been a second edition, and now, this re-published edition. It was a privilege for me to be married to Steve during the time I wrote this book. He was the center of my life, and I will always love and miss him. During our 30 years of life together, we ministered in hundreds of churches around America and in many parts of the world. In every church we found the same thing, good people who love God, but have been hurt and are crying out for healing. Today, this same issue afflicts many believers and non-believers alike.

So many of us have been crushed by the pressures of life thinking that God is mad and paying us back for something we have done in our past. The truth is that God loves us and wants us to bring our wounds to Him for healing! Thus, Encouragement Ministries!

Even when we love God with a passion and strive daily to obey Him, there will still be times of confusion and desperation in life that will make us feel like God is silent when we call upon Him.

God continues to use Encouragement Ministries, Inc. to minister to the bruised and broken lives around the world. God is able to give us hope, healing, and strength to overcome the difficulties in life through the love of Jesus Christ our Lord.

To schedule a booking or for more information about Encouragement Ministries, Inc. please go to: www.LanaBach.com